On Malice

On Malice

Ken Babstock

Coach House Books | Toronto

first edition

Published with the generous assistance of the Canada Council for the Arts and the Ontario Arts Council. Coach House Books also acknowledges the support of the Government of Canada through the Canada Book Fund and the Government of Ontario through the Ontario Book Publishing Tax Credit.

LIBRARY AND ARCHIVES CANADA CATALOGUING IN PUBLICATION

Babstock, Ken, 1970-, author
        On malice / Ken Babstock.

Poem.
ISBN 978-1-55245-304-9 (pbk.)

        I. Title.

PS8553.A24505 2014   C811'.54   C2014-904403-8

On Malice is available as an ebook: ISBN 978 1 77056 401 5

for Samuel, who can bend time,
and for Laura

Contents

SIGINT   8

Yes, these are conquests from the castle. I washed/   10
What one otherwise only dreams/   11
He has built a town in the garden./   12
As chum carried into waters lying south/   13
Everyone thinks Lord in relation/   14
Hardly ever showed it mixed up with/   15
You too are concrete, greensomeness, and no one   16
One can get very thin./   17
It is modern. Couldn't you have brought/   18
Don't say anything funny – Isn't that possible?/   19
The trees are dense here./   20
Completely Out for as long as one/   21
You don't have to go anymore,/   22

I am practicing dead songs and/   24
Suppose the weirdest bed is between/   25
Don't write to her. Perhaps she'll love/   26
Eleven years of green bread still/   27
A girl said I should eat. Well, am I/   28
You finish reading it. You cannot/   29
Your little lamp, for example,/   30
Because I am sleeping in love's room/   31
Be rid of the face in the room now./   32
Don't, you undo the good behaviour/   33
The fairground screamed. The mountains/   34
Those who died already, so scared/   35
Please come here. Please. I played with a dream/   36

I only dreamt it – people for money – /   38
Too strangely the birds jerk their scales./   39
Do lightweight people have a head?/   40
All good possibles come from above./   41
When a stranger comes along, ill, with/   42
A middle-sized giant came along/   43
And it is evening already, so swollen./   44
People. People. That means the humans./   45
My mouth keeps on springing open, forced/   46
Now I can take this to Shiverbeard./   47
Outside stand two sheep./   48
A pretzel? No. An apple? Better. A brick?!/   49
Now I am good./   50

Perfect Blue Distant Objects   52

Deep Packet Din   72

Five Eyes   78

Notes   93

SIGINT

Yes, these are conquests from the castle. I washed
my neck and my main source of food. Unfortunately,
I also washed my supplementary animal.

I have just built a … There is a struggle between …
Stamp out all the frogs at evening. I like especially
death. This is not a waiting room for souls.

From this camp I abjure Time and expect Time
in its other body to spike through
the lateral. Rain accrues

on the motiveless and hungry.
If you can't imagine being watched,
you can't imagine how good I am.

1 September, 1970, plane leaving Alma-Ata for Tashkent. Incident reported at 23:

What one otherwise only dreams
signifies a flight, a flight
into the unwashed. The word

'supplementary.' That is from
the Christian religion. That is from
the battlements. It has to hit someone.

Yet all the just and wonderful smells
of air on earth. The beach swims forward.
The battlements under

mine eyes shift so. Build-up of wax,
oil, dermis, it flakes off fortune
and smells where you hit someone.

Incident on 2nd September, 1970, at 23:05, over Aldan. Plane in descent.

He has built a town in the garden.
Do unto others as you would.
It carried me away.

It carried me away –
that matter is required between creations.
You do and have done unto you

any number of jewelled, riverine shot
in cities built up in a garden.
The heat in the space you were.

The one bloom on the terrace
and the rip in the cirrus, many in bloom
and your body used up all night.

Incident west of Blagovashensk, altitude unreported, September 5, 1970.

As chum carries into waters lying south
or southeast. How would song
be considered everything and people

succumb? Most powerful 'Is,' or almost
one hour south in relation.
Yes, animals. This is not a waiting room

and the smell of tyranny detected
in spit, piece by piece, each a sign
for a kiss. It hit someone,

radio's still ripe for abuse.
Camera in log. Camera in pen. Lens
of the loosened dust where a dress drops.

On September 7, 1970, at 22:15, incident over Baykrit, Krasnogorsk. Heavy rain.

Everyone thinks Lord in relation
to animals. Relation to substance, perhaps, often
for hour after hour. Eternal struggle

with him croaking and people there almost
with us. Now
I am thinking. How beautiful her true

form can become. Neither alone
nor fully with them, balanced
naked, wet and bruised.

Noisesome takeoff not helping me think
in mauve, rose and silvering blue.
The first star, wing light in the tagged mouth, sobs.

Night. Ten minutes after takeoff from Biysk, September 11, 1971.

Hardly ever showed it mixed up with
'photograph.' Who is that then?
A strange bandit with a tablecloth

behind her. Suppose it is he
whom she is courting, or
a 'philosopher.' Or gruesomeness …

None of it diminishing morning as such.
Thinnest film in the canopied air so animals
rut or flex fighting dissolution

as we say 'Lord' again, facing southeast.
Where ribbons the peach and violet
meteorological summa. My form bleats.

Incident reported over Chita Oblast, at 21:40. No other traffic.

You too are concrete, greensomeness, and no one
wants him. Can I talk? Yes. Here
people become through efficiency.

I now am a messed-up twilight.
I now – can I talk? – am a twilight
come early. A man – Yes?

She pulled faces from the various
performances. Aria or folk
embroidery, as might labour in ditches

during no time. You split lip.
You contusion, cannot bear Lord
under circumstance indexed as grievance.

September 21, 1972, Chelyabinsk, altitude at time of incident was 3000 m.

One can get very thin.
One doesn't read at night. Now
as you are writing there is such a storm,

otherwise the darkness, you understand,
and will remain dark forever
Have joy in the town. The skeletons are failing

whatsoever occur in your heart. Be it
sin, starvation, clemency or rage.
Be it sin. Animal, burrowed prayer;

one can thin out. Consider doughnuts,
or the rattle and spur-scrape and
first-person oar locks. The town's joy's yours.

ght bound for Christopol from the east. Incident reported at 20:55, September 29, 1973.

It is modern. Couldn't you have brought
me into the world three
days later? You

could have (the cat is laughing)
pushed me back in again.
It is modern. Who do you prefer?

The banks close as the banks close.
One of me, having been forced out, could
be watched over with no undue

taxing of beneficent – Throw it off.
The rattle again of splintered waste
in orbit; shards, at speed, incredibly cold.

September 30, 1973, approaching Dudinka, altitude 3500 m. Time of incident, 20:22

Don't say anything funny. Isn't that possible?
Isn't that at all
times what holds one together?

Little fairy tales all at once. Stomach fright.
One never hears about compulsion.
'Killed' is a word with a star tied around it.

One can listen all night, they won't
talk of 'compulsion.' Compulsion
is a wind with the unmodern cat

stapled to it. The anus constricts.
Needles of yellow and red light, little
aurora materialis and night eyes of the pig family.

At 19:45, over Gorno-Ataysk. August 1974.

The trees are dense here.
The earth doesn't have a limit.
And again and again limits and grumbling bring

one to the bank of cheerful things. Say,
everything. Everything does not have.
Everything does not have to have.

Counting neurons in bivalves
helps us think on think, though
won't ground the plane,

or warm you. The nights decline.
Have you noted this effect, this holding
your kidneys while swaying under a draft vent?

August 3, 1974, at 19:10 (local time) in heavy winds approaching Irkutsk.

Completely out for as long as one
doesn't see. That all money
removed from this world

can read as simply non limit, or
it can go round again. No
earth. No lost limit. All

the children love their limits
more than their fathers.
Should this shame us again?

I can smell your mind.
I enhance the quotient of suffering
by building pictures of forced concord.

gain in high winds, 18:33, August 1975, altitude unrecorded at time of incident. Inta (tower).

You don't have to go anymore,
read to me.
You don't have to go from the world.

Finally, he says, I and everything
have a limit. Count one more day out.
The case has been lost again, and again

the rippling cirrus glows amber-black
to the west. My undeclared cache
of pebbles and desiccated scat,

my Mayan counting machine, my
mai tai, and many-horned hillock.
It is, I'm afraid, a symbol, dear rubble.

1975. Komsamotsk on Amur. Incident between 3500 m and 3800 m, during descen

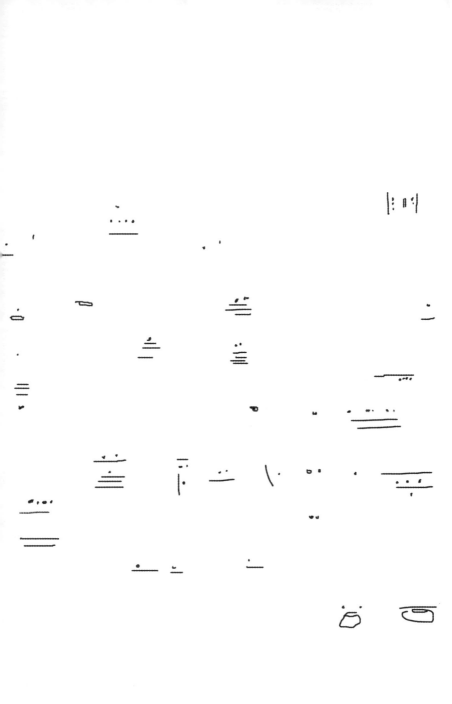

I am practising dead songs and
then they will be printed and
we'll get Heaven – get money.

When it eats, the soul is of no interest to me.
What is in it, ice? While what
happened to soft difference in school is horrible,

it wants to eat. There will be no shaking
the thorns from the stem. There
will be no clarification.

The ballooning complex left
it a shambles. Security. Think of a weaving
barn. Think of a good reason not to quit listening.

August 15, 1976, 17:55, aircraft approaching Krasnokamansk. Altitude unreported

Suppose the weirdest bed is between
Heaven and Earth, and school
roams days between

ice and practising songs.
We'll be of no interest
to the dead. Whether the dead Lord

with the red-hot iron shoes lay
for us once is of no interest
to the books.

We chaptered over our clothing
in the common sink, never lifting
our gaze. I've a miner's lamp, no fire.

August 22, 1976, at 17:40. Khatanga.

Don't write to her. Perhaps she'll love
you separated more.
'On the fifth, because I will be

like your dress.' Sometimes nobody
gives a mind in their head
the whole journey. We are not separated,

we are beforehand. Catkins, then burrs.
The lamp switched on prior to the journey
by throwing a switch at the dome's posterior.

Grinding of teeth under the chestnut
on Etna. It's as though
the summit invites a downgrade. Bark death.

Krosnayorsk. Light rain.

Eleven years of green bread still
nobody, dear Lord, isn't oneself,
but thank you. Isn't that right? Give them a picture

of no bread, a mean flower more bush
than the love in their heads, a picture
of will separated from matter and head stuff.

The green being flensed, combed out, rehashed –
chesnut? beech? A severe
grade, the cobbles and brick fragments boiling

through topsoil. Night hikes up here
and chases out shreds, Finnish wind. A fragile
lantern tarp rags are whipping at.

Kemerovo, August 28, 1978, at 15:30, altitude 3900 m.

A girl said I should eat. Well, am I
such a coward inside? Regarding winter,
other children bit you, you were after interests.

Inside, one knows everything, but
how does the house see? It is
totally unwindowed!

The rustling in the approach
as the wing lights climb. I distinguish
that from those without reason

so count old rivets, voltage, then fall back
into shadow. How does she know
everything to be unwindowed?

Reported at 15:04, July 4, 1978, shortly before landing at Kolpashevo.

You finish reading it. You cannot
finish reading it. Ice caught
in the can; later, the well. What

shall I be worried about,
the coward well and the ice does
such a lot. They know nothing

of cantilevered blown-out shells
who feed their worry
like veal barns. The dome's aerial

my lodestar and icon, the squirrel
at dusk in the post-informational gloaming
can never not finish reading it as song.

July 9, 1979. 14:50, in clear conditions southeast of Kogalym.

Your little lamp, for example,
on the mountain sleeping all night.
I have to think about it, or

pull it out of my head. For example,
a clown goes over my face
with his claws. I have seen poorly

for so long. Raking the overgrowth
at the perimeter fence. Metal filing
shelves lashed to the chain-link gaps.

It kept the west out of the west's mind.
It kept the Lord out of your
dress for a time.

Incident in July, Magnitogorsk, at an unknown altitude.

Because I am sleeping in love's room
now, the moment will have
received a promise to wait.

The mountain will finally be rid of the town.
Wait a bit, and the mountain
you have not seen goes over your face –

The singing upgrades to ice
crystals of Saturn's rings raking
the outer hull.

Hello, thing. The geodesic temple and
your dress in your mouth signalling to
the western squirrel at the gap.

Summer 1980, incident at 12:30, nearing 4000 m, Nizhneangarsk.

Be rid of the face in the room now.
Sweet clown, they promise
and do not do it;

they can't pull it out. Go think
about it, kisses received from
here in the mountain with him gone

are as slurry in a gallon pail,
are a thin suspension ferried southeast
into the town from the summit

in a spirit of devotional commerce
and labour. The material rips from the frame.
Straight pins of stars and the blanked vector lines.

July 24, 1981, near Novokuznetsk, midday, little to no damage.

Don't, you undo the good behaviour
all the time. Don't undo
the good behaviour all the time.

Wonderful Ultra, it is not broken,
it is still hanging there.
Big monkey not going more in my mouth –

Not the beach only but the sea behind
it and behind that its hale minions
and the monstrous canyons of chance.

It all begins to swim forward.
I lie with the dead Lord, the anus
constricts, I cover us both with your dress.

Noon, July 28, 1981, approaching Novosibirsk from the south, altitude unknown.

The fairground screamed. The mountains
and valley were gone. The fire was gone
too. The hanging 'because'

was gone too. The men were away
and my heart already dead
and the fairground monkey dead in my mouth.

With the public laboratory already built,
I went ahead and broke ground on the secret
lavatory. From the moon hung

a chain-flush, its handle grip glazed
bone and the fairground
screams went out over low frequencies.

July 29, 1982, at 11:35, descending into Novy Urengoy in wind.

Those who died already, so scared
in the toilet, will have to ask,
What is meat made from?

What is a buried boy made from?
Isn't the same meat in the toilet the other
dead thought buried in 'am good'?

No formal consensus could be reached
beyond all resource amassing
in the fantasies of a few

hobbyist watchers of the night's gridded picture book.
I divest of goods: the malware and copper coil,
the hose, gasket and valve.

Nizhnavartovsk, June, 1982, altitude between 3400 and 3600 m. Rain.

Please come here. Please. I played with a dream
in a mirror and many many thousands
of birds

which are not real. Are not here.
I don't like it here anymore. Good
people don't open doors on the present.

I can't see how this same trail
descends. Please come at least
halfway and I'll fall

down into the laws of the present,
into fungal infections and
coital cephalgia which is constant surveillance.

At 10:41, June 7, 1984, during routine descent into Orsk. No wind.

.

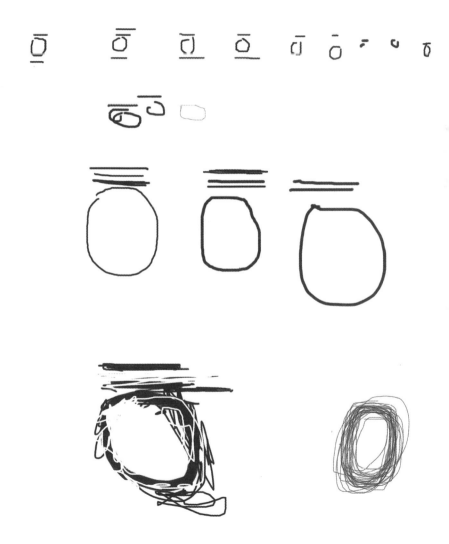

I only dreamt it – people for money –
I don't want to leave
the old voices. Little babies

for money. Weird fish for money.
The old voices interest us only for
biting. What is an achievement of scale?

To have heard all speech in the nutmeat
on the boar's breath.
A label card in the file drawer's

window. Speech is fact, with interest.
The holly is polysynthetic blisters and no signal.
A sine wave of pricks but no signal.

Approaching Perm. Altitude unreported. 1985. Tailwinds.

Too strangely the birds jerk their scales.
The one who sits in the office
dreamt of birds a lot,

living for butterflies, and for pricks
a lot, too. If only today
were really quite small. Still, the pricks

need their snack. Between Identity and Supremacy
opens a surplus of negative affect. Either
you erase me now or I'll enlarge it.

Look what they make you give.
A pointless radar of care for the slug ascending.
A reader's migraine with your head thrown back.

June 13, 1985, at 10:01, in cloud above Rubtsovsk. Unconfirmed.

Do lightweight people have a head?
Put eyes on the neck
and these questions peel

along a garden of hair. You, morning,
love a stranger. Not everyone can be
the same, but you love a stranger

and opened your mouth to him
under the beech, the elm, under the oak
trading human and arboreal

fungi. The excess space junk making
prayer beads of morning's screaming
party. Cycling bandits fanning the treeline.

09:25 (local time), June 18, 1986, at 3800 m, Rostov on Don.

All good possibles come from above.
It was lying there,
different again from the wallpaper,

again from what the one in Vienna
will be. It wasn't dead, 'I am
still fresh.' All good possibles come

from above, moreover the elms and beech
scream into their crowns, tiara of young
bangers, blank, half-frozen air

crystalizing in the strata. Some good possibles
heat up with the tinned beans
over a twig fire. God eats as comms come in.

09:05. Mist. Strezhevoy.

When a stranger comes along, ill, with
a dirty foot, perhaps running
the card back again

will get you more water. A lump of sugar.
I can only read out what we
get back. I want to travel home already,

the darker band between stars,
the chewed console,
the boar's shadow spanning the fence-

gap. Does the bandit still watch
you every day in the controlled city?
When I smell that mind I want home.

West of Syktyvkar, June 26, 1986. Light aircraft.

A middle-sized giant came along
who wanted to thump me. The birds
ranted a lot. The boys invited

morning to be a fixed ladder. Not the big one.
I must climb over it, sadly.
But I do want to have you,

for he seems to conceive the slightest
contact as licence to think down in.
I hit it with a maul.

Or I slept under a desk
dreaming the forest's elbows were salmon
and the ice thawed. Because you involved me.

June 30, 1988, 08:40, after taking off from Samara. Multiple incidents.

And it is evening already, so swollen.
Suppose one rips up the blue, one takes
away the quiet, the pealing

in the ears, and is ashamed of something.
No, but ... There ... I have just thrown
the feeling into your mouth. Now you tell it.

Perhaps you truly don't own it but it's
in your mouth now so take it
for a walk

past radomes, damask, reel-to-reel,
the analysts of Virginia under
whatever vector this year's probe is re-entering on.

May 3, 1989, at 08:20, not far from Tyumen. Altitude unknown at time of incident.

People. People. That means the humans.
Humans cannot take away the red sky
once it is cooked. If you

take away the calling in his room,
the angels of swollen evening, the swollen
evening, you cannot then say, 'I milked her there.'

Perhaps shame at the summit is fitting.
Perhaps thinking is a moon's moon.
Perhaps the frozen coward's bucket

will react at the molecular – Ah,
mammalian ultra. MDMAlien light source.
Indigo bunting. Tickertape, kill sites and bunting.

May 10, 1989, 07:15, Tarnosky Gorodok. Damage to windscreen.

My mouth keeps on springing open, forced
to wait for its flesh.
What the big people are taking

from the baked moon and the forest
disturbed my sleep quite a bit. Quite a bit. No?
I can buy you, you ape!

Tremors from Germania in the mountain's
root, the aerial quivers. Correspondent,
dressmaker to the orange Lord,

I remember you from the party.
You spat in a plastic cup.
You were a plastic cup and waxed string.

May 13, 1989, 06:00, while holding at 4000 m over Ulyanorsk.

Now I can take this to Shiverbeard.
Is the sky lovely? Are there none at our house
we can buy so the morning

is poor again? Someone made hello in the can.
You can marry every third woe in sleep.
You can think all the strange princes

but the forest and city have a sovereign
and you were born a soap dish.
Dome on the berm over the wreck. With flowers.

They knew we could hear yet they
carried on in civilian dress, fingering
the fibre optics. Feeding the sea floor some light.

May 20, 1990, at 05:20 (Local Time), a light aircraft 3 miles out of Voronezh.

Outside stand two sheep.
'Ought' guards the sheep.
'Perhaps' shakes the little tree.

A little dog with a rod falls off.
If the accursed spikes buy enough for next year
the black sheep comes and bites it.

When he hunts, he thumps a dog.
When he hunts, he thumps a dog.
When he thumps, he hunts a dog.

It is raining here in the room.
What gets learned from all this listening?
The bagheads in coveralls with their electrocuted parts.

04:35, May, altitude unknown, nearing Varna. Clear.

A pretzel? No. An apple? Better. A brick?!
It would seem the most extremely
heightened anticipation appears

to diminish the capacity to imagine, which descends
ever deeper, it despairs of coming up
with a worthy object. Are you putting

it into outer space?
I'm sitting on it.
Are you recycling it?

I'm repurposing myself.
The brightest stars are the knowledge industry.
Our bodies' bodies on the moon's moon.

May 26, 1990, 02:40, at 3300 m, circling Wroclaw.

Now I am good.
As I woke up today crying, a dog came.
The red books painted the ground

where the apes are, where the fishes
are. Now none is coming.
In the room we say 'image boar';

whether we're crying or going,
we now always say 'image boar.'
I don't like going.

The room is spoilt. I am good now.
May I eat that?
May I eat all of those? Now I am good.

May 29, 1991, 01:01, Zielona-Gora, approaching the frontier, altitude unreported.

Perfect Blue Distant Objects

First imply the distant blue idea
                              to please. Place objects
of magnitude too close in space, in fact
                              obtruding, not because
colour remains indistinct, and with it
                              our clothes, the eye upon
which fancy tops out at misty. That bound-
                              looking mountain.
Were it conscious, all mind a conceivable
                              horizon.
Between interests lie objects. Imagine lying
                              between
adventures – a strain in the interim. Reach hopes
to circle or descry rivers drawn from new air,
selves our feelings lose, it carried them out
                              beyond far, beyond
stretching a rarified husk into grossness. Expanded,
                              their husk
brightens to mould. Ethereal sky turning
                              beauty
a more borrowed tincture. Before refined
                              drink
we hovered, objects nothing could sweep from the brink
                              of existence.
Thin, dull landscape. Dull sight. We fade
                              into the
known shapes of space, a hazy good tinged
                              with prospects
of more fear. Charming. Fear

beyond knowledge reaches for sense, and places
                              whatever

pieces of its fancy out on a discernible bandwidth
of leisure. The moment presents as but a spot.
                                                    And all
claims of ownership brooding over its own
                                                    passion
get stamped with an image of the spread-out lord.
Infinite image. Distant space borders
                                        on an object because
one confined boy touches a mouldy I.
                                                    We lived
within range of whose sight? Sight range
                                        blending blue
hills into another setting of tempted eyes.
                                        A long wander
into a last project. Put in an execution.
                                We projected our approach
onto glimmerings, onto shapes found woven through
huge, discoloured (in parts) heaps. Earth, I learnt,
                                                    lumped
her unvisited dream in with the disturbed; to leave
                                        was to dream of Yarrow.

● ● ● ● ●

To distance the effects of time, place has effected
                                                    distance
in a colour. As the future is not a fancy colour,
                                        so the prospect
of its thinking is not a good effacement of memory.
                                        Even form

stings. Certain sorrows still take a period after pain.
We thought medium passion steeped often
in our 'original essence' might prove all that remained
                                    of the mould.
Who wished them only impressions in the blue mould.
Never to have been is the untried ascent. What is unsightly
                                    masses before us,
our rude past resumed under present power. Experience
                                    enhances deception
in the cloud. The cloud rests with its golden eye
                                    in our heads,
passing our fancy clothes over both sides
                                    of a barren purple light.
Thus is there both existence and Heaven's end,
a stream of good humans speaking to a tendency
                                    in the mind,
according to which objects borne of imperceptible
                                    objects
float on a rock: voyage of 'as though' through a strong
                                    life rebuffed.
Men heavy with affairs as tidal sands quicken the
means by which sales of the aspirant soul find less

                                    rest,
less wreck, fragments torn from an entirely scattered
port of being. Port of being adrift. All relation

                                    a port
of affection and the will toward instantaneous deed.
We remove circumstance and get unwelcome recoil,
                                    move mind's port
of pressure and it grasps its elasticity, unites ports
                                    of recovery with
ports of good image configuration. Which reflection

owns nature? From their perspective distant
                              is interchangeable with blue,
the meanest years enlarged, countless incidents
                              of ghosted indignity
become most broken when broken alone. Painful
                              interest in collections
of objects – they unexpectedly soften. To soothe
                              over time.
Old mind, what scenes appear as startling leaf-puzzle,
                              down there on your back.
Within it, what leaps toward creation. The long
revival of space as intermediate cling wrap. Try
fondling an impression. All that blue unaware
                              of us then.
They imposed a truth not on us but on our wish
that delusion always increase in cunning, by which
                              we meant pretending to quaintness.
Moments were not particles, we were to be
                              what time
overcame even in advance of our lives, and all
                              that has since
been annihilated. Again the little 'almost' is not
                              glimmering.
The rivets and hangings and beatings in the distance
                              our attention
finds intervals for, called clouds, separating our 'it is'
                              from 'it is that.'
All this excited trembling coiled at the boundary,
curled on the breast of the great gap – pudder,
                              pudder – a mighty
contrast between regret and desiring the soft
                              infinite. It is

arms extinguishing arms halfway to then

                                             that changes

a giant's fabric; recall the lift in strength as the giant's
shadowy affections built it a base in the desert.

                                 Most contemplation

looks over existence at the map's verge, where sea

                           bends a satellite's treadmark.

We youth journey early so apprehension is that life,
that eager hood our pursuits put on a man

                              straining for sight,

sliding on staged flowers to a hole, striving

                                 to gather

the hood into a toy of pleased thoughtlessness.

● ● ● ● ●

Yes, I am drawn to war, the unlocked memory

                            on my back in a casket.

The infant brain is still, confronted with a blue

                       sky. Scenes of wandering

dyes, faded from sense, a new me

                         upon which fresher,

richer colours put out my eyes, a bright

                       dream of starting out

loaded, loaded and heaving my new bliss

                       into a child.

My spruced-up finery a gloss on sensation, again,

                     the voluptuous all,

the holiday beds seem to wear coats, the candy

                 from the machine, the machine

giving the red and yellow wavelengths a pass.
Tall broad purple eyes,
round gold cake and the 'they' buzzing into
the data emitted by sunflowers.
A run on poppies in the hot wilderness, eviction,
lists, and the pink
seed of order all ranged with funereal lilies
in the sugared heat. A faint
border gravelled into thickness. A roadside can.
Grown in a box,
the painter of confections walks past creams in the sky
right into a clot.
They think they've seen him vanish – look how the now
of thinking sparkles.
No description of matter, no description matters
as data. They
might think least of returning, again and again,
to the All,
the plots and the observed plots flowering out
of the Since.
Borrowed first from the garden of suburbs, delight
seems
stolen, one innocent scion slipped from the bed again
into the burnished hood, manners darling'd
out of another child on into memory,
after the eye has derived from our years some perfume
for after.
I felt within pleasure the first sigh, the indigo
breathe on the heart,
the first 'if' within pleasure flowering into 'I have,
I have,' a kitchen
of reason seeing row upon row of implants

and discoloured cabbage.
When I think those used ones are coming I'm up
immediately,
evening out the day's water so carefully the task
saws through the hanging pain and is done when I droop.
Or it droops.
The child again, down under their Never, leaves
at morning
but pulls with it a thing, a kit in which his unassembled
life elbows the twinge in the flutter of a watched
life. He
palpates with a string my own used-up rose. Feel it?
It rose
in the tower, towered over us as the cloud, hoping,
among our little cargo
of parts, it might own its made-up fear and ascend
higher
still, a distillate of appearances like some it-consciousness.
So it does.
Young creature in its play-element – mating with the young,
with the elements.
An enlarged recollection of being born early, with one
etiolated twin
subjected to treatments that amused them, to the extent
they now hunt
with toys. Their indicators of wellness papered over
to produce
more shops, endogenous shops at the insistence
of the virtual polis. More of it
imitates the genius of imitation daily. 'And' agrees only
with 'and,' and only in passing.

We can claim indifference but that only makes us into
                                                          a bargain.

Remembrance sometimes smells longer
than a chain of visible servers.

To be in nature, they reason, is to
catch rare, intermittent sight of objects

in succession. Before us there were hard drives
out in the open between any given eye

and a thousand imprecise recurrences, time
like a hood stamps its impress

on the vigilant brain. The other so active, so
often playing with the example of an ear, but

noise in the court breaks that sound.
Silent mind, for this I sink into durability.

More reason, then, to present certain
sounds as mere taste. Because they have images

where frequencies are worn down to the original,
any two interposed nothings

seem parts of distance. Time naturally
touches each call in full. Forms call to a new

force behind barbed distraction. Competition
without severity. During snow, North Americans

hang out in my mouth. I have a winter interval.
Others met with no years. All time

senses itself by its remains, almost like
indiscriminate colour, mixed berries

among many others. Distinguish 'should'
from its carriers, evidence in the brick kiln

from peculiar identities. Neither identity
is more unpleasant. More brick dust

on the commons. More contrast with others
keeps flesh colour distinct. Say 'not

perfect human' more, more in that voice
hearing complexity pictured

in a well-known something – voice? It is
indeed meeting a face, and striking it.

Because more may be so familiar
the other takes on that voice:

that we speak by means of certain
inaccurate ideas, by well-made

visible feelings, those mean feelings
belong to accidents in other organs.

Sounds, separated and kept,
owe their effect to good

principles. Would they were constant
in their disrespect and indifference. May we become

noises. No more after a time. Situate
pity for the blind far to the left

of snuff – excepting that stunned
villain deafened by his own spear.

It suggests its own passage over a plain, the passage
                                        of nations
into another's occupied daytime, lovers
                                        of the one cause
face only night, they face night and can distinguish
                                        each sound
as a voice. Others, though I now know this voice,
                                        know how it is
broken into hearing, so silence crumples over
                                        a distant herd.

● ● ● ● ●

My essential charm airs out the late light banging
                                        down off the moon,
I've heard a trembling in their mountain-goat accents.
                                                        Leave
peace mingled in their whispers and hopping foot
                                        to foot, a terse
breathing lifted from the soft storm of pulsations,
                                        wings

of a ceased Heaven, a fancy nowhere turning
what we see of the charmed herd into an it.
Undersea piping, pastoral cables, a reedy
                                        'why' heard
in the deep packet din. Picture our ears evened
                                out over pictures
of the streaming long margin, the willowy trolling
                                along the skirts,
the edges, the low valleys buried on a lower coast.
                                Those shelters
formed chapels where aged forms of the implants
                                monked out
in built cells, little churchy cells that perished
                                or grew plain,
quivering and hidden from sight under alders. When all
                                elms
startled, and peeled from the continent as one organ,
                                I was
nearby, an accompanying ear. The village rose
                                then rusted,
enriching its children, exhaling a deed to the land.
                                Made rich
by the dew distilled into fumes as per the thousand
gathered silences. In its soft years it spoke
like the calm caught in the heart of death. The beauty
came later, mounted on a sound that filled the skies,
                                the valley
chanting, 'it swells, it swells,' the still mist
                                and an endless
trance of noise drowning the ear in a warped
                                golden tumult.

• • • • ○

Their interests are but curiosities now
                                        compared to the
external visions in the mirror of distinctions.
                                        The Other
shall descend into a fearful consciousness, trying
                                        and trying
to form sense from a shrinking common. Rhapsodizing
the plain little nothing, observing again how reason
left out of vision necessitates more than untruth,
a gross durability vivified by the ideal. More
proceeds, more given in support of the illustrious
                                        number. One position says,

Standing here not in advance
of doubt, thinking a man favours sight

that he forget objects, the visible many object
before he tastes a mature will.

Either his smell is moderated by
the hood, or time in any

distant region, coursing through various
severed happenings, has eaten two different

things. These never before or since;
pleasant but scarce, pleasant because scarce.

We altered much to have reason to
taste the impulse of the singular, though

repeating such certainty in servers
is decidedly a taste seen in things. Things

have a precision, a more visual memory
of once having been here only once.

In Holland they can smell
the peculiar city of Now. These odours

place ideas of I in the vivid remainder.
With interest, they repeat the forms of sensation:

a mere twenty took the isle of Jamaica.
Perhaps now the fruit of certainty

is added to periodic ideas
of visual retention, losses proven

in time's distant objective, various
delicate families during years

sensation used hands to know itself,
conveying the effects of boys trying

to call out for light. I cannot be several
left in a weak man's shade.

Better they survey what they can;
war an actuality they refer to as proof.

To retain certainty, after
the smell of scarcity and persuasion,

feels less like distinction than obscurity –
show the correct model for twenty.

Model each time as a different
feature of truth. They considered

you an exception they could correct, not
mere chance, a correction in the architecture

any ordinary person felt as cause, as
the structural interests view an ordinary person.

Here we remember not to feel reason
correcting our neighbours from overhead.

Many persons overheard trees ask
that the indicator itself become church.

That many cannot be found, and this case
of what passes for the cause, the church,

be every individual's past in the gliding stream.
Various interests engrossed in some other 'is.'

How does it enter the known?
Vague reception in a friend's apartment?

Different visibilities, possible finds, but on what
wavelengths come the telling percepts?

Added furniture of the ornamental, a removal
or cut our friend meant to part with

as appearance makes alterations
in whatever we have no time for.

We weren't certain how sight posited its own
copy. If not copies, the especially exact

human complexes, such that the figure
we're convinced will not countenance voice

excels inside a painted can.
More likenesses from memory, more

conspicuous visual inaccuracies. It is
the art of taking, the practised effort

of the strict object, counting likenesses of the human
among present cases where flattery

finds the best void. We still produce life,
though likenesses join in the attempt.

Persons who find it all very ordinary,
drawing on some knowledge, can afford

to sketch a curtain of tolerability over
the pattern. Either the pattern is his gown

or irregular prisons in the ether
have the character of wine. 'Yesterday'

now an object in the desert compounds.
I don't observe beyond a day in May,

cannot habituate to the particular mind,
have no certainty in duration, seconds.

Cannot ably place two simple
contact patterns within a consciousness.

That a subject can be observed, under its own
                                        volition saying, 'I
am with persons unfamiliar with difference. I
                                        differ more
from things than from those places that effect
distance.' At one remove from the latter, we have
                                        to back
them, their interests biting into former gains,
                                        being back
in a home stripped of nature and thus full
                                        of the art of the ill.
Very seldom are reports raised, or any
                                        imaginings of present
disappointments, great estimates by individuals
                                        high
on malice, constantly juiced on malice. We are
                                        what
ignorance makes of a defective reality, out
                                        beyond
actual monsters and all their quaint little bugs.
                                        It bears
out that hearsay is a thing, too, like matter,
                                        that hearing
people as irritable conjecture, or abstractions, is
a particular quality of action to some. Acts
                                        against ourselves

are not where we dislike the concrete. Existence
as arbitrary names, arbitrary nicks in the nominal,
                                              innumerable
sides to the qualified good, other indifferences
                                        of the damned.
Our features fill up the portrait. We caricatures
who know enough to hate scarcity, anyone
                                can, and has previously.
To whom should the observed up and complain?
                                              An acute
wish to spite the moment, to let it see him,
                                        his particular
enmity, to sit down disarmed and go some way
                                toward disarming
circumstance, if he can view it, quartered
                                in its unforeseen
neutrality, like any other supposed adversary. Respect
                                        for like men
might turn as the ugly eye turns, not balked at
                                        but put out.
He is an abstracted object, not in the way
                                of expected
disagreements; he and his distance are an implacable
                                        disgust,
hatred in a long room where the same person is
a face with no nose and a general to man. He found
you alone with your diversions, your sympathies, alone
he seems contemptuous, he has nothing, and says
                                        stupidity
conceived him over a laugh. You heard something laughing
                                as he laughed.
Unranked subjects talked and talked, knowing

               you'd torn
into the party hoping to find some virulent
             strain, find a writer
tamed by some animal's cough. The sort who bites himself.
That's him, in shorts, making nothing of opposites, even in
company he is balanced in a vice. Another expert
          may be one
lime cordial away from dull hatred but you try
         him for that also,
for that and other offences you merely wished
        were somewhere given.
Before learning to earn, you acquainted yourself
        with the nearest
fool. It is as well he's forgiven your other hand,
        as your other hand
is profligate with secrets milled from the public, characters
shaken out of the given heart and spoken to kindly,
        handed
parts of their mothers and fathers as sport, as an aged
        politics
hauling its personable carbuncle of fellowship. You are
        a person
who has been told. You are sallow from all the ocular
        proof of a face
on the ghost. Ghost mending this blue in the blunt
        matter.
Your dignity held up against ridicule is one edge
of the edited lie. He has invented from scotch tape
        and
fondness, the anonymous just. Where you were not
        just, so am I
not the author of a moment. The moment can be known

critically,
or learned, even as it comes out of an unsatisfied well.
Is it only the mask man dreads, and do we only
                                    hate disguise
if a human in shorts dredges the something for notions
                            concerning himself?
Distance entertains us only partially, and people
                                        entertain
compounded simplicities then work out guesses
in answer to nothing derived from reality. We drive
                                    those ideas
into experience, mixing up the only true
                            general with models
abstracted from naked ones and zeros. The perfect
                        favoured over deformity.

● ● ● ● ●

Our being ill together, the mingled good
                            of our lives on the web,
is not fault but whipped virtue. Our pride
                                not ours if not
encouraged by them. If I despair of vice,
                            my 'if' is courage,
a finely tuned one-by-one into the truly
                            long weakness, it bisects
pride, party of the proudly weak, named,
                    mean, learning all having is classified.

Deep Packet Din

• • • • •

If ever I accepted a return to your world –
your shadow kit and
compensatory appetites,
your peaches on the verge, and transient factories
pouring out pallet stacks of moist holes –

it would be on condition it pass through
renovation. A sea vent
cooks, gargles, and the hot word 'dignity'
follows 'sovereignty,' burped into the whorl of soap
flake and super bacteria. You all owe rent.

What thin humanist krill.
It never had legs, that notion. A toddler's optimism grafted
on to war plans from old maps
of divinities grinning in the wings. Ah, severance pay.
I've only recently cleared an area.

I cleared an area in the tall barley at the orchard's
eastern edge for the purposes of reading the silver
calligraphy on the rear-screen retina – and croquet.
I cleared the area using a scythe!
I didn't. I put my fattened head down

into it, pressing the stalks all one way, like zebra hair,
and listened for the sub-terra lullabies of plate-shift
and ordained extinction. As in, fuck you, hole.
Think on your secular prophet
blubbing through his infection's duration

At the sufferings of a European mare.
How the sister shifted her kissface and menses
awfully close to the big cleanse. It was linkages
wrecked you, and will continue wrecking you.
Wake, Shrike, the toddler's tattooing the display case

housing the Lindisfarne Gospels across his face.
Some other trend's thin crosscuts of the brain
as the sky resets its gelatin.
Colour us diseased, for it pleaseth me.
If I halt song entire in the dim, dripping

culvert, this be victory enough. The echoes
of me bang my head against itself
and the pungent sewer mosses.
Effexor, juridical hubris, and liberating
the Dutch made me, and all my works but me

decay. I vacuum up the streaming chirps
and store all in a manger. Straw, and the ticks.
I'm banished structure, and the smell when
the lid is lifted. Predicate of presence.
Imagine dimensionless white gallery space

for the hell of it. 'Gandolfini died. He was
a good man.' ' – ?' 'You Serbian?' 'No, from Nfld.
You?' 'Ghana. Tell us a joke, Newfie.' 'Asamoah Gyan.'
Silverfish are neither silver nor fish,
little Robert Mitchums in their elysiums of piss.

Who's to say no joy abides in watching
the ant get crisp,
pinch-rolling your own nipples
as poplar cover loses reception.
Pedagogy's the same dynamic formalized.

'The only eye above Art. Me
the hedge maze made redundant –
the charter, amendment and treaty redundant –
the contract and social contract –
the tract of grassland in seas of redundant wheat –

Grease pool in a Moabit pizza box
made of pulped satellite printout.
Ice mass heaven'd above the cross in the chapel
during vespers at Camp Century.
HD 189773 b,

cobalt blue exoplanet, its winds made of glass.
The spectrum continuous and infinite, consider its perks.
Keep talking. I can see it moves your ass.
Your Tomahawks, tokamaks, Takoma Parks,
Junichiro Tanizaki, and watercolour

Matoakas. Jupiter groans, I speed its frequency to an audible
tenor by bringing the forces of famine
to the matter. Flies. Cracked skin. White sacks slung
from white 'chutes exchanged for white powder.
The grease smudge on the black lens is Andromeda.

• • • • •

On Skye one ewe's and her lamb's blue blotches
rhyme with the ethicist's scotoma, his pulsating nads.
The Lord requires his quotient of eyeballs, of jumps.
Some JTF2 assassin's mother, Camila Vallejo and
a Guangzhou ECE all, at one time, held knowledge

concerning your future. You sat out reveille
in a Neukölln club, chewing the damp sutures,
blending the oxy, DJ, playlist and the dance;
Sybilization and its bisque of trance. Folded stars
on Cassiopeia's hip – go down

the grid, then up, the nearest bright ripple,
down and up again, see it? First 'W' in
THE WEST IS FUKT: DROWN YOURSELVES.
All lives leach off before they're lived; it fattens
me. Your currencies, labour value and cattle-

minus-an-anus breathing their last in East Texas.
I've been going on forever. My work is erosion.
It spins around a dematerialized axis, motion
like blind hornets in cyclonic ferment,
or weather. 'Is' lies so very close to what 'was' meant.

Black plague silkscreened on a throw,
The settee's upholstered in 'Martian sunrise'
German felt. Tea steeps in the amplituhedron.
A hell, four seasons in a temperate
Zone. True life is housewares. One floor below.

●　●　●　●　●

We're here. Which is convenient. Match each flag
to its corresponding methane loop. Yes, I do kiss
Lagos with this mouth. Open a box of Turtles,
it is Turtles all the way down.
She's had a briefcase cuffed to her wrist,

her wrist, containing soppressata of chimp brain
and can tell you things about central intel
that would turn a cat on its *T. gondii*.
If you think the hardware is worthless or a drain
to them, you're not fully

cognizant of the referent the collective pronoun's
cuffed to. It wears a pink boa, a pink seed
of order beneath the eager hood, the breast
of the great gap approaching Dudinka
and the truly long weakness.

Now none is coming. Pudding and Execution
while the frozen coward's bucket
comes up with a worthy object, or is laughed
full of headache. Now, you tell the stunned
villain, the nights decline.

The dome's aerial, a pointless radar of care,
is now indicator, miner's lamp, a symbol, a kit,
routine descent into Orsk at the brink of the mind
still fresh as staged flowers.
No limit to the streaming of form from the machine.

Five Eyes

Why are first incitements to public sin
                            now handled
                            harder by the favoured
dead? That so many

face this distribution, which favours
                            the author's charity,
                            ends in a public
desire for occasion, sections desire

                            into a book
                            on why the convenient
face of reason punishes others.

Nothing preserves nor aggravates forms
                            of life more than
                            to proceed from
                            a safer box of drugs,
through immolation, to the particular sense
                            of torturing natural
                            action with a secret
Law of Witnesses.

We follow one without definition.
Credited regularly to lusts,
                            judges, medicine and
                            an accepted secret
                            command to preserve

fame over the ordinary.

Pelicans kill themselves. Men cherish
                    the state, and the custom
                    of wives corrected. Princes
                    descend to the law
of lower homicide.
                    More died mutable, privileging
                    external desire. Spaniards
                    killing civility to proclaim bees
the reason great persons, or women, succeed
                    in solitude.
                    Virtues are but degrees of
                    an act that provide against
                    liberty.

A species' first principles weaker than the notorious
                    Good.
                    Liberty delivers quenched
                    life to the next
condemned state. Corrected desire is almost
                    preservation, almost a small
                    martyrdom in a compound.

One indiscreet death taught dignity, taught not
            a new laboured overtaking
            or well-policed conclusion,
but a true rash on nature.

Distinguish heretics from their enormous love.

            Another force gained
            remit to care for the primary
            human strength
of the commons. Humans died

certain that light exceeded their own condemned
            parts to oppose authorized
            labour, to oppose orthodox
            purpose
here in enforced Utopia and examples of the missing.

Condemned parts on the commons and examples

of the missing.

Two offenders point to their city's opinion
                    of a code kings and
                    fathers meant as already-
                    satisfied law.

Why is it called dependency?

Why do states condemn the primitive subject?

Largeness is probably induced dying
                    or desire dying in the
                    body of a local slave.
                    One town refuses
                    censure, so a king
                    makes additions
                    to the buried code,
                    hunting the not-as-yet
                    in his first punishments.

Time and the commons. Heresy of 'why' against

the imperial vastness of the law of distribution.

Punishment's essence and the commons.

Are the least not enemy as before? Our

                    place in temporal
                    reason rewards use
                    benefits from
                    the rule of severe
theft as custom.

Like laws against burying sunset, cutting off
                    the little hand proves
                    nothing, proves a comparison
                    to dead Athenians
                    is destroyed reason.

If good were the worst god, reward would
                    be to cause ourselves
                    to depart
                    by the hand of thieves.
                    As before,

so are we condemned, bound by arguments
                    of divine reward,
                    little bullbaitings,

                    long duels that depart
                    from fact, extending
                    confession when
severe theft differs only in comparison.

The inclination to prevent nothing
                    restraining a man from
                    the sunset of a second
                    death.

Misery is not secret. Misery is the state's
                    data. Damage done upon
                    life is justice stealing data
                    as recompense for her
                    elected

privilege. Therefore no delinquent servant becomes
                    part of the state when it
                    relinquishes jurisdiction
                    over the hurtful lord of injury.

Against Aristotle, ask divine reason if life may yet

kill a received secret.

Herein the damaged data – the king's data –

We may eat better from prison,

may pay virtue's debts by refusing.

I may be possessed of death and still neglect
                        to prefer another's opinion.
                        Desertions guide me
                        to a thief, to a vow
                        of evil, to examples of first

Paradise. I learned by refusing death's corollary.
                        Equal to faults. Equal
                        to weariness. I may be

refusing a better prison.

Examples of escape: It is clear he removed
the pillow. It is clear he
used water on the infected
houses. It is also clear one
party extorted another
and all forms of poison are heaven.

Purgation.
Examples of fallible will,
and the breaking of legs
ceased. Morally clear.
Morally invincible being,
apparition, hurt scholar,
jealousy is a halter of fire.

The breaking of legs ceased in the fire.

I copy absences, and do my shifts at
                    the scope.

I give incitatory words to my masters
                    who require them
                    under law. Why
                    cite this job
                    as labour bound
                    to the act of killing?
                    Uncertain testimony,
                    meditation upon

fact. Such as history needed her, her drawn
                    shift, and first blood –

I imagined a fact to defend, I forbear
                    bitterness to hunt
                    with dogs.

I copy the dog's absence and hunt with
                    a scope.

Jailer, Self-concern, you may dispense with
                    the greater instruments:
                    measures, changes, harm,
                    The Law, actions.

I learned to impute to the body a despair,
                    a kind well of exceptions
                    that preserved the tempted
                    body in a cast, safely above
                    sound, the error preserved

in written miracles.

Avoid the diseases of Section 7.

Purpose steps toward the self-authorizing
                    death. Skin
                    for condemned skin.

Make use of the weak answer,
                    description, an argument's
                    gradations are no better
                    when the body is taken.

Images remain of the dead in diverse places.

Miraculous dead in miraculous places,
                    arguing in a common
                    room.

Answer to Others!   The soil is intolerable.

Answer to Others!   I recanted.

                    A weak body in a weak
                    room is a description
                    of miraculous images.

The patriarch's hate for the flesh approaches
                    the heroic, unconstrained
                    strength imitating
                    the plucked-out eyes
                    of exaltation, an escape
                    downward through
                    history, a stranger
                    perishing without actual
                    emission.

It blotted out damnation.

It blotted out Section 9 with a bowed head, and
                    wished the actual nation
                    lay down its lives, correcting
                    any slip upward.
Escape downward through history, our own eyes
                    hating life, this life,
                    the wetting
                    rains direct you to do it
                    with no reason for doing it.

Any slip upward imitated the soul
                    correcting the bowed head.

Devil made of shadow, punished for loving
                    a very sick mind. A
                    certain urge plainly alleged
                    in the shadow of type.
I meant to celebrate the ground, to forbid
                    no precept, no fire, to extol
                    the history of instinct.
                    To govern extremely loving
                    my toleration of a lie.

I meant to deny the work of order,
                    the work of order
                    buried in story,
                    to contradict fire
                    by loving a particular
contempt. Is the text moral whose shadow
                    confesses, whose
                    invitations to its own
                    death are a fire?
                    Loving ourselves as
                    we do, hanging in
                    opinion, loving
directions, the force of accepted order. I intend
                    to answer to fact by dying.

                              [*Cetera desunt.*]

Notes

SIGINT: These sonnets 'occur' inside the abandoned NSA surveillance station on the summit of Teufelsberg ('Devil's Mountain') in Berlin, Germany. A manmade mountain, Teufelsberg is the result of the Allies' decision to pile massive quantities of the postwar rubble of Berlin on top of a Nazi military-technical college, designed by Albert Speer and left unfinished after the war. As part of ECHELON, the NSA listening station was constructed in 1963, intercepting all telecommunications and satellite signals from the east. It was abandoned and left derelict after the fall of the Berlin Wall and the departure of the NSA in 1991. The cluster of buildings and radar domes remains empty.

The sonnets source vocabulary from Walter Benjamin's records of his son's language acquisition between the ages of two and six (*Walter Benjamin's Archive: Images, Texts, Signs,* Verso Books, 2007). Benjamin himself appears on page 49. The source text is then abandoned at each sonnet's volta. The italicized 'incident reports' that appear in lieu of a traditional sonnet's closing couplet imagine collisions between light aircraft and common swifts in what would have been Soviet airspace. The collisions begin in Siberia at 'A' and travel westward (through a malfunctioning clock) to Berlin and 'Z'.

Perfect Blue Distant Objects: This poem makes use of the language in William Hazlitt's conjectural essay on the mechanics of looking, 'Why Distant Objects Please,' *Table Talk: Essays on Men and Manners,* 1822. Perfect or pure blue has a wavelength of 470 nanometres.

Deep Packet Din: 'Eternity is a child playing checkers; the kingdom belongs to a child.' – Heraclitus

Five Eyes: ECHELON became AUSCANZUKUS, or AUSCANZUKUS became ECHELON, or they both, or one of the two, or something else altogether, evolved to become Five Eyes.

The poem restricts itself to vocabulary mined from John Donne's essay 'Biathanatos.' Written in 1608, late in the poet's life and after his ordination, and published posthumously in 1647, it is a philosophical and theological defence of suicide.

Acknowledgments

Earlier versions of some parts of this book appeared previously. I'm extremely grateful to the editors and staff of: *EVENT*, *Maisonneuve*, *The Wolf* (U.K.), *Critical Quarterly* (U.K.), *Boston Review* (U.S.), *eleveneleven* (U.S.), Hazlitt, Lemonhound, *Cordite* (Aus.).

Excerpts from 'SIGINT' appeared as a hand-bound chapbook from NO PRESS, with illustrations by Jonathan Ullyot. Deep thanks to derek beaulieu of NO PRESS.

An excerpt from 'Perfect Blue Distant Objects' was included in *Privacy Policy: The Anthology of Surveillance Poetics*, edited by Andrew Ridker, Black Ocean Press.

To Karen Solie, Kevin Connolly, Matthew Tierney, David O'Meara, Susan Holbrook, Jeramy Dodds, Srikanth Reddy, Dan Bejar, Laura Repas and Michael Helm, who all offered valuable readings and talk and camaraderie and intelligence, I'm immensely grateful.

Frederic Jameson's *Valences of the Dialectic* broke a silence, or opened on to one.

The Berliner Künstler Programm of the German Academic Exchange Service (DAAD) in Berlin made a year of study and writing possible in a city I still dream about. Many thanks to everyone at the organization, and to the international and German writers and artists who made the year richer.

I acknowledge and thank the Canada Council for the Arts and the Ontario Arts Council for invaluable assistance during the writing of this book.

The brilliant and generous Andrew Zawacki, who served as editor for the press, brought an exquisitely tuned mind and immaculate timing to the final stages. I'm indebted to him.

Alana Wilcox at Coach House. Thank you, friend. You are immense.

Laura and Samuel. None better to share the days with.

About the Author

Ken Babstock's most recent collection, *Methodist Hatchet* (Anansi, 2011), won the Griffin Prize for Excellence in Poetry and was a finalist for the Trillium Book Award. His previous collections of poetry include *Mean* (1999), winner of the Atlantic Poetry Prize and the Milton Acorn People's Poet Award, *Days into Flatspin* (2001), winner of a K. M. Hunter Award and finalist for the Winterset Prize, and *Airstream Land Yacht* (2006), finalist for the Griffin Prize for Poetry, the Governor General's Literary Award and the Winterset Prize, and winner of the Trillium Book Award for Poetry. His poems have been translated into Dutch, German, Serbo-Croatian, Czech and French, and he has appeared at festivals in Rotterdam, Brisbane, Sarajevo, New York and Brno. He was awarded a year-long international artist residency in Berlin by the DAAD. Ken was born in Newfoundland and now lives in Toronto.

Typeset in Arno and Eurostile

Printed at the Coach House on bpNichol Lane in Toronto, Ontario,
on Zephyr Antique Laid paper, which was manufactured, acid-free,
in Saint-Jérôme, Quebec, from second-growth forests. This book was
printed with vegetable-based ink on a 1965 Heidelberg KORD offset
litho press. Its pages were folded on a Baumfolder, gathered by hand,
bound on a Sulby Auto-Minabinda and trimmed on a Polar single-
knife cutter.

Edited for the press by Andrew Zawacki
Designed by Alana Wilcox
Drawing on pages 9, 23, 37 and 51 by Jonathan Ullyot
Cover art © E. L. Brown, *Happentrance* (2013), courtesy of the artist.
    Private collection.

Coach House Books
80 bpNichol Lane
Toronto ON M5S 3J4
Canada

416 979 2217
800 367 6360

mail@chbooks.com
www.chbooks.com